MW00964706

Wise Men
Seek Him

A Christmas story
by Elsa Henderson

Xulon
PRESS

Wise Men Seek Him
A Christmas story
by Elsa Henderson

Printed in the United States of America

ISBN 9781613792933

www.xulonpress.com

Wise Men Seek Him

by

Elsa Henderson

Forward

Mystery: The ancient Chinese acknowledged a supreme God, *ShangDi*, phonetically similar to *El Shaddai*, for whom they had no image or idol. The Early Zhou pronunciation, 'Zhan-dai', is even more similar. Some Chinese characters have an uncanny way of telling stories in Genesis. How did that come about?

What did the Chinese know about Genesis and the one true God?

Fact #1: Many Chinese Christians believe that one of the wise men who visited Jesus in Bethlehem was an astrologer named Liu Shang from China. Liu was the surname of the emperors in the Han Dynasty, during which Jesus lived.

Fact #2: The only Old Testament reference to a star is in Numbers 24:17 – words spoken by a sorcerer named Balaam.

Fact #3: The Bible does not tell us the names or the number of magi, only that they were from the east and brought three very expensive gifts. Various cultures have theories about the number of magi, their names and where they were from.

Fact #4: Magi followed a star to Jerusalem and then to Bethlehem to worship the newborn king of the Jews and bring Him royal gifts.

How did they know what the star signified?

Fact #5: Though our current calendar purports to begin with the year Christ was born, we know that early dates are someone's best guess. King Herod died in 1 BC or 4 BC, depending on whose calculations you use, so Jesus' birth was before that – probably 3 BC or 6 BC.

Fact #6: The Magi were not at the stable with the shepherds. They arrived somewhere between 40 days and 2 years after Jesus' birth. Joseph and Mary were in Jerusalem for their purification 40 days after Jesus' birth (Luke 2:22 and Lev. 12). Herod killed young boys 2 years old and under (Matt. 2:7, 16) after enquiring diligently of the Magi as to the time the star first appeared. Joseph took his family to Egypt immediately following the Magi's visit (Matt. 2:13 -15).

Can all these facts be reconciled?
For the purpose of this story, I have used 3 BC as the year of Jesus' birth, as the arguments for that date are, to me, the most convincing.
Here's how it might have happened:

*Israel's last stop before crossing the Jordan River
from Moab (modern day Jordan)
into the Promised Land
1406 BC*

B alaam saddled his donkey and headed for his home in
Pethor, near the Euphrates River, penniless and in disgrace. He didn't look forward to the three-week journey.[1] He knew the return trip would seem a lot longer than the journey that had brought him here to Moab.

. . . .

Balaam had been born in Ur of the Chaldees,[2] the centre of priestly learning for magi known as Chaldeans. As a Chaldee, Balaam was familiar with Moses' book of Genesis, stories of the patriarchs, and Yahweh, God of Israel. He also knew about Israel's exodus from Egypt and their wanderings in the desert.

But Balaam aspired to be more than a mere priest with a good education in Hebrew holy books and the right to make sacrifices to Yahweh. Magi in other centres were not simply priests and wise men but astrologers and magicians. They consulted the stars and spoke in peculiar 'tongues.' Kings consulted them on difficult subjects for their 'learning.'

Those magi who were most successful in predicting the future or in invoking blessings or curses were paid handsomely for their ability to manipulate the gods.

With his education, experience and knowledge of many languages, Balaam realized that if he played his cards right, he could be rich! So he left Ur and travelled to Susa, the capital of Persia, to study under a poet-prophet-priest named Zoroaster.

Balaam and Zoro had a lot in common and became instant friends. Zoro had a genuine thirst for knowledge and a brilliant mind. He studied astrology from the best, and became an astrologer of the first rank. He also had a gift for poetry, a flair for the dramatic and a canny knack for saying things that would induce his hearers to pay him well.

When Zoro's students proudly claimed that their prophet's name meant 'Golden Light,' Balaam only smiled. He was aware of Zoro's humble beginnings; he knew that Zoro's mother had been a milkmaid and that 'Zoroaster' was more accurately translated 'owner of feeble camels'! That Zoro had been able to convince his students that his name meant 'Golden Light' only endeared him to Balaam. If only *he* could be so convincing!

After a few years of studying with Zoro, Balaam left Persia. He felt he had learned all he could from Zoro. Besides, Zoro seemed to have cornered the market for well-paying students. Maybe Balaam could find rich patrons in Babylon. If not, he would learn more tricks of the trade from magi in Babylon and then move on.

When Balaam and Zoro parted, Balaam was surprised to hear Zoro thank him for all he had learned from him. Balaam thought *he* was the student and Zoro the teacher!

Eventually Balaam chose to live in Pethor. It was located on the border between modern day Syria and Turkey, just west of the Euphrates River, on the highway going east to Haran and north to Turkey. He was only two days' journey from the crossroads of the world, the international highway that connected Babylon and Egypt with the ends of the earth.

Balaam's bread and butter came from serving the community just across the river in Paddan Aram. They were mostly believers in Yahweh and employed him as their local priest. The people of Turkey, just north of where he lived, were also receptive to Yahweh and the teachings of Chaldees.

But Balaam's talents appealed to other religions also. He quickly made a name for himself and soon had customers from near and far paying him well. Occasionally Balaam heard a still, small voice telling him that he was trying to serve two masters, but he let the clink of coins drown it out.

One day a group of princes from Moab and Midian arrived at Balaam's door. King Balak of Moab had watched the Israelites as they wandered through the desert countries on their way to Canaan. When the Amorites in the territory just north of Moab had refused the Israelites permission to pass through, the Israelites had fought the Amorite army and defeated it, capturing and occupying all their cities and leaving no survivors. King Balak feared that his country would suffer the same fate, though the Israelites protested that they were merely traveling through on their way to Canaan. King Balak even went so far as to recruit help from the Midianites, who lived close to the Red Sea – almost as far south of Moab as Balaam was north. The princes of Moab and Midian, speaking on behalf of King Balak of Moab, were offering Balaam a handsome fee in return for pronouncing a curse on Yahweh's people, the Israelites.

Balaam blinked when he discovered how serious King Balak of Moab was about cursing Israel. Yet the princes offered significant pay for a task simple for a Chaldee. Swiftly Balaam recovered his composure and in true sorcerer's form told the princes he had to consult his god first. Then he ordered his servants to bring the best food and wine and make sure the guests were comfortable for the night.

Balaam went to bed dreaming of how he would spend the money and completely forgot to consult Yahweh. But God came to him, asking, "Who are these men with you?"

Balaam had never heard Yahweh's voice before, but he quickly recovered from his surprise and explained the situation to Him. God replied in no uncertain terms, "Don't go with them. You must *not* put a curse on those people, because they are *blessed.*"

Balaam was not one to be easily intimidated, but he shook at the sound of Yahweh's voice. The next morning he reluctantly told Balak's princes that Yahweh had refused to let him go. As the princes disappeared out of sight, Balaam mentally said goodbye to what should have been easy riches.

As the weeks went by, Balaam's fear of Yahweh faded and he began to resent the God who would deny him the wealth he craved. The more he thought about it, the more Balaam resented both Yahweh and His people Israel. He kicked himself for turning down King Balak's messengers.

To his surprise, Balaam was given a second opportunity. Another group of princes, more numerous and more distinguished than the first, arrived from King Balak, offering a much larger fee for divination. Despite protesting that he could not go beyond the command of his God Yahweh even if the king offered him his palace filled with gold, Balaam offered the messengers a little crack of hope.

"Stay here tonight as the others did, and I will find out what else Yahweh will tell me."

To his delight, God said, "Go with them." Balaam barely heard the rest of it: "but do only what I tell you."

In the morning Balaam got up, saddled his donkey and went with the princes of Moab. But God was very angry. He sent an angel to stand in the way. The donkey saw the angel, but Balaam didn't, and beat his donkey mercilessly.

When the donkey spoke to her master, Balaam was so angry that he didn't even notice, and replied as if he were talking to an ordinary human being! Only when Yahweh opened Balaam's eyes to see the angel with his sword drawn did Balaam understand the peril he was in. A fearful Balaam continued his journey with the understanding that he could speak only the words God put in his mouth.

King Balak met Balaam at the border of Moab and scolded him for his delay. Balaam did his best to keep the king happy. Twice, in two separate locations, Balaam went through his sorcery rituals only to end up blessing Israel.

Finally the king of Moab took Balaam to the top of Mount Peor, from which they could see Israel encamped tribe by tribe on the east bank of the Jordan River. There the Spirit of God came upon Balaam and he spoke words that would become seared into his brain: *"A star will come out of Jacob; a scepter will rise out of Israel."*

King Balak was apoplectic! Not only had Balaam blessed Israel, he had cursed all the surrounding nations – *his* neighbors! Balak sent Balaam away without so much as a crust of bread for his return journey.

As he headed for home, Balaam was at first relieved to have escaped with his life. He even treated his donkey kindly. But gradually his relief turned to resentment and then to anger. The closer he got to home and the further from Moab, the more Balaam was obsessed with the thought of riches lost.

Some time later, Balaam received news of what had happened after he left. While the Israelites were staying in Shittim, east of the Jordan River, their men began to indulge in sexual immorality with Moabite women, who invited them to the sacrifices of their gods. The people ate and bowed down before those gods and joined in worshiping the Baal of Peor. As a result, Yahweh's anger burned against Israel, and He sent a plague which killed 24,000 Israelites.

Balaam cheered when he heard the story. Then he had a brilliant idea. He could still profit from King Balak's offer of riches!

Early the next morning he saddled his donkey and once more started on the long journey to Moab. By the time Balaam reached King Balak's palace, he was bubbling over with excitement.

"I know the secret to defeating the Israelites and driving them out of your country," Balaam told Balak. Balaam then recounted the story of what Yahweh had done to the Israelites in Shittim.

"Don't you see?" Balaam said. "You don't even have to lift a sword. All you have to do is get the Israelites to worship your gods and indulge in what their priests look down on as 'sexual immorality,' and Yahweh will be so jealous that He will destroy Israel for you!"

"Are you sure it will work?" Balak asked skeptically.

Balaam was so sure that his idea would work that he told the king, "If it doesn't work, you don't have to pay me one shekel."

"If it does work," Balak said, "I will pay you double my previous offer."

So Balak instructed the priests of Baal Peor and the priests of all the other gods of the high places of Moab to actively proselytize the Israelites. They invited the people to feasts where the food had been sacrificed to idols, and they seduced the men of Israel with their temple prostitutes. At the feasts Balak laughed as he told the story of Balaam, who had uttered oracles in the name of Yahweh yet had sacrificed to the gods of Moab along with Balak. Mockingly, Balak repeated Balaam's oracle in the best sorcerer's tradition:

"The oracle of Balaam son of Beor,
    the oracle of one whose eye sees clearly,
the oracle of one who hears the words of God,

who has knowledge from the Most High,
who sees a vision from the Almighty,
who falls prostrate, and whose eyes are opened:

"I see him, but not now;
I behold him, but not near.
A star will come out of Jacob;
a scepter will rise out of Israel."

Balaam had continued to prophesy that Israel would conquer Moab, Edom, the Amalekites and the Kenites. He even said that ships from the coasts and islands of the Mediterranean would subdue the mighty empire of Assyria but come to ruin against Israel. Confident that that would never happen, Balak dismissed Balaam's prophecies as the over-the-top incantations of a sorcerer.

But Yahweh had the last laugh. Balak had not taken into consideration what Israel had learned during forty long years of fighting for survival in the wilderness. Shittim had been the last straw. Israel had learned, at least for the time being, that they did not want to be on the wrong side of a jealous God who would drown Pharaoh's armies for opposing Israel, yet who would not hesitate to wipe out Israelites by the tens of thousands for worshiping other gods.

In his last military campaign before turning over the reins of leadership to Joshua and before climbing Mount Nebo to die, Moses sent 12,000 men, one thousand from each tribe, against the Midianites for their part in opposing Israel and seducing them into idolatry. Without suffering a single Israelite casualty, they wiped out all the Midianites who had come up to Moab to join forces with King Balak. They killed every man, every woman and every boy, leaving only young virgins as survivors.[3]

A post mortem revealed that, "in addition to those slain in battle, the Israelites had put to the sword Balaam son of Beor, who practiced divination."[4]

So ended the 'wise man' who sought riches rather than God.

Near Xi'an, China,
the capital city of the Han dynasty,
1400 years later...
12 BC

Liu Shang shivered in spite of his thickly padded garments. He had spent the entire night searching the heavens, as he did every new moon when the sky was clear, but he had not seen anything new or unusual. New moon, when the sky is darkest, is the best time to study the stars.

Then, shortly before dawn, just above the horizon, Liu Shang spotted a comet, clearly visible to the naked eye.

When the sun rose and he could no longer see the comet, Liu Shang ran to tell his grandfather, who had taught him all he knew about the stars, but now was blind. Grandfather Liu got more and more excited as he questioned his grandson in detail about what he had seen. He asked repeatedly about the intensity of the light.

"It sounds just like the comet I saw 76 years ago!" his grandfather exclaimed.

For several nights thereafter, even though Grandfather could not see, he sat wrapped in blankets beside his grandson while he watched the comet's progress through the night sky.

Liu Shang made detailed records in the star catalogue which he would later turn over to the emperor. Grandfather Liu talked at length about what he had seen long ago.

"All the astrologers considered the comet's appearance to be very auspicious," Grandfather said. "It was first seen on the night of Emperor Wu's 70th birthday. The astrologers said the comet was evidence of heaven's blessing on Emperor Wu of Han. He died the next spring while still on the throne, having ruled well for 54 years."

Once Grandfather got started, there was no stopping his eulogizing of Emperor Wu.

"Emperor Wu was the greatest emperor of the Han dynasty," Grandfather said, "in my opinion, the greatest emperor China has ever known. He had great talent and bold vision. He was a master of military strategy. He drove out the Huns, who were always trespassing on Han territory. His conquests extended China's borders beyond that of any previous dynasties. He maintained and extended the Long Wall of 10,000 Li,[5] referred to in the West as the Great Wall, to keep the Huns from returning. No wonder the descriptor 'Wu', which means 'military force', was chosen to characterize his rule and became part of his title!

"Under Emperor Wu's rule China became one of the most prosperous and powerful nations in the world," Grandfather continued. "The political stability he brought to the country paved the way for splendid achievements in the arts and sciences, as well as our economy and our foreign affairs. His supreme achievement was building a vast network of roads which connected with pre-existing highways in the west, giving access to the Mediterranean Sea. As a result, caravans of camels now can move with relative ease and security, enabling us to trade our iron and copper, salt and silk with people in places as far away as Baghdad, Antioch and Alexandria. Within a few decades all the ruling families of Rome were anxious to attire themselves in silk, and the entire transportation network became known as the Silk Road. As long as the manufacture of silk remains a Chinese secret," Grandfather said, "we will continue to be enriched by the silk trade.

"The prosperity derived from the Silk Road and international trade produced a new class of gentry who had the wealth necessary to become educated. Many encyclopedias were compiled during Emperor Wu's reign, containing everything known about geography, animals, plants, philosophy and popular myths. Sima Qian, China's greatest and most famous historian, over a period of 58 years wrote his

Records of the Historian, which provide a detailed chronicle of China's history, from the first dynasty to the Han dynasty, ending with the death of Emperor Wu.

"Thanks to the prosperity Emperor Wu generated," Grandfather said, "all of his relatives – that includes me – were able to get a good education. Even your education, Liu Shang, generations later, is thanks to Emperor Wu."

"I am forever grateful to Emperor Wu, Grandfather. I can think of no better position than mine – to be able to spend my life studying the stars and the writings of wise men. When I am not studying the heavens, I am studying the writings of our historians and philosophers."

"And what have you learned from them, Liu Shang?"

"I learned that Emperor Wu is not solely responsible for our country's prosperity, Grandfather. The First Emperor of Qin, the dynasty which immediately preceded our venerable Han dynasty, had the foresight to order that all carts must have axles of the same length. That uniformity made it possible for trade to flourish throughout the whole empire of China. The Silk Road was a natural extension of what he began. He also standardized our written language so that our characters are consistent from one dialect to the next, even from one language to the next. We Chinese can communicate by writing even when we cannot communicate by speech!"

"Ah, yes," Grandfather replied, "but the absolute power that enabled the emperor to unite a fractured country under a tightly centralized government was also the emperor's downfall. Military rule is effective for expanding an empire, but unworkable for governing in peace time. That is why the First Emperor of Qin was the only emperor of the Qin dynasty."

The conversation drifted from history to philosophy.

"What do you think of Kong-fu-tse, Grandfather – Master Kong, the one westerners call Confucius?"

"He was a great thinker and philosopher, a great moral teacher," Grandfather replied. "Confucius was not widely accepted during his lifetime. It was only during the Han dynasty, about three hundred years later, that he gained status. In the first year of his reign, Emperor Wu made the works of Confucius required reading. All chancellors in the court had to learn the Confucian classics before they got a promotion!

"Confucius put great emphasis on the importance of study. He wanted his disciples to think deeply for themselves and relentlessly study the outside world, mostly through the ancient writings.

"Confucius' writings themselves cannot be considered a religion, though he did champion Chinese traditions and beliefs both old and new. He made a number of allusions to ShangDi, a heavenly power who was worshiped widely during the Shang dynasty, but he also championed the more recent practice of ancestor worship, and he stressed that children must respect their elders. Confucius advised sacrificing to spirits, not because he was convinced they existed, but because he felt it wise not to neglect or despise ancient ceremonies which might contain some truth."

"Until I started reading Confucius, I did not know that others believed in ShangDi," said Liu Shang. "I thought I had invented the name ShangDi, the Emperor Above. It was the only name I could think of for the one who made the sun, moon and stars that I observe so carefully."

There was silence between grandfather and grandson for a moment. Then Liu Shang posed a question he had been pondering for some time.

"If even a man as wise as Confucius could not be sure of the truth, how can I know the truth, Grandfather? I have been studying ancient writings, but how do I know they are *truth*? That is why I love to study the stars. They are not the expression of someone's opinion. Sometimes I wonder if they are trying to talk to me. I would love to learn truth and gain timeless wisdom from them."

"The search for truth is a noble search, Liu Shang. I also seek the truth."

"If only I knew where to find it," Liu Shang mused. "Sometimes I think I would travel to the ends of the earth to find it."

"Thanks to Emperor Wu and the Silk Road, such travel is now possible," Grandfather pointed out. Liu Shang nodded thoughtfully.

Grandfather continued with his thoughts. "Confucius said, 'Every legend contains a kernel of truth.' Maybe you should begin your search with the study of our legends."

. . . .

Grandfather Liu died the next winter, but his words continued to influence Liu Shang wherever he went and whatever he did. A seed had been planted in his mind.

If legends contain a kernel of truth, Liu Shang reasoned, then truth must predate the legends. He determined to search the earliest documents he could find. If that didn't lead him to the truth, he would travel to other countries in search of it.

. . . .

From information gleaned from writings on 'oracle bones,' Liu Shang learned that as far back as the Shang dynasty, China's second dynasty, the king, in addition to his secular position, was considered to be the head of the ancestor- and spirit-worship cult. He presided over highly developed court rituals to propitiate spirits and to honor sacred ancestors. When the kings died, they were buried in royal tombs at their capital city of Anyang along with articles of value for use in the afterlife. Sometimes hundreds of commoners, presumably slaves, were buried alive with the royal corpse.

What kind of gods, Liu Shang wondered, would be so cruel as to demand that people be buried alive? Surely the God who created the beautiful night sky would not be cruel. He created the sun to give us warmth and light. That is good!

Liu Shang continued his research. He studied Confucius' writings and discovered that all of Confucius' *Five Classics* included references to ShangDi. According to Confucius, the Chinese belief in ShangDi predated even China's first dynasty.

ShangDi was not only the earliest god on record in any Chinese narrative literature, he appeared to be unique and superior to other gods, Liu Shang discovered. ShangDi literally means 'the Above Emperor' or 'the Heavenly Ruler.' Loosely translated, it means 'Lord on High' or 'God Most High.' ShangDi was sometimes referred to by the name Tian, or Heaven, implying the presiding God of Heaven. Unlike subsequent gods in the Chinese pantheon, ShangDi was never represented with images or idols.

What did he look like? Liu Shang wondered.

Liu Shang was fascinated by the fact that, during China's third dynasty, even though other gods had been added into the Chinese belief system, philosophers believed the right to rule came from ShangDi. They taught that the ruler governed by divine right under the Mandate of Heaven. If the ruler was dethroned, that would prove that he had lost the mandate – that he was no longer the 'son of heaven.' This doctrine explained and justified the demise of the two earlier dynasties and at the same time supported the legitimacy of present and future rulers.

5 years later...
7 BC

While Liu Shang was wondering about ShangDi, he was invited to attend the emperor's 'Border Sacrifice' to ShangDi, an annual ceremony held during the winter solstice at the Temple of Heaven complex in the Han dynasty's capital city of Xi'an. The ceremony dated back to the first dynasty, and was the year's most important and colourful celebration.

The Temple of Heaven complex contained architecture unlike any other. The three temples to the gods of the sun, the earth and the moon, like most buildings in China, were rectangular in shape. Each corner of the roof was upturned like a hook to catch any evil spirit flying by and prevent it from entering the temple. Along each ridge of the roof was a series of ugly creatures designed to scare away evil spirits.

But the Imperial Vault of Heaven, the temple of ShangDi, was circular! It had no corners or edges, no hooks or ugly creatures – only beautiful, smooth lines. Its blue-tiled roof, representing Heaven, was topped with a gilded ball.

According to Chinese symbolism, Earth is represented by a square and Heaven by a circle. The circular Imperial Vault of Heaven stood on a square yard, Liu Shang noted, symbolizing the connection of Heaven and Earth.

Inside the Imperial Vault, Liu Shang noticed that the entire building was supported by eight pillars. In the centre of the Imperial Vault of Heaven stood a shrine where the wooden tablet of the God of Heaven was placed. The characters on the tablet were too faded for Liu Shang to read. He wondered what had been written on the tablet. Was it a prayer to ShangDi, or words from ShangDi to man?

The Temple complex was not unique to the Han dynasty. It had been patterned after a temple complex in the previous dynasty which had fallen into disrepair. Because each temple was built entirely of wood, it eventually disintegrated and had to be rebuilt – roughly every 200 years. If a new dynasty established a new capital city, a new Temple complex would be built there.

Liu Shang watched with interest as the emperor meditated at the Imperial Vault while costumed singers, accompanied by musicians, intoned a prayer to ShangDi, then the emperor sacrificed a bull on the great white marble Altar of Heaven.

Liu Shang paid special attention to the content of the prayer. In it the emperor addressed ShangDi as his Maker, expressed great humility and reverence toward him, and promised to observe all his rules and statutes. ShangDi was obviously very different from other gods, for the emperor prayed, "We worship Thee, *whose goodness is inexhaustible!*"[6]

The other gods certainly were not good, Liu Shang thought. They were to be feared! This ShangDi to whom the emperor prayed appeared to be more like Liu Shang imagined he would be. ShangDi, according to the emperor's prayer, was considered to be not just the controller of the sun, moon and stars, but the Creator of the world! "Of old in the beginning, there was the great chaos, without form and dark. The five elements [planets] had not begun to revolve, nor the sun and moon to shine. You, O Spiritual Sovereign, first divided the grosser parts from the purer. You made heaven. You made earth. You made man. All things with their reproducing power got their being."

Then the emperor continued with a prayer for a good harvest.

When Emperor Ai had ascended to the throne at the age of 20, the Chinese people at first were excited because they viewed him to be intelligent, articulate, and capable. Soon, however, he proved to be corrupt and tyrannical, an incompetent administrator, a womanizer and a drunkard. The people showed their displeasure by giving him the title Emperor Ai – lamentable emperor!

Liu Shang shared the same family name, Liu, with the emperor; they were distant cousins. He was aware that Emperor Ai did not really believe the words he was saying in his prayer to ShangDi. Emperor Ai was superstitious rather than religious. He believed in ghosts, and went through the motions of the Border Sacrifice ceremony only for good luck. The people expected him to make ritual sacrifices to deities, spirits and ancestors and to act as the highest priest in the land. It was believed if the emperor did not do so, he could disrupt the fine balance of the cosmos and cause calamities such as earthquakes, floods, droughts, epidemics, and swarms of locusts.

The Border Sacrifice ceremony was so out of keeping with what Emperor Ai believed that Liu Shang could not help but wonder. Where and when had the ceremony originated? Why did the emperor sacrifice a bull? What did the writer of the prayer know about ShangDi? Liu Shang determined to research further.

Texts written on wooden tablets, bamboo strips or silk cloth were relatively recent, Liu Shang knew. They were not more than 500 years old. The oldest documents he could find were oracle bones – tortoise shells and flat cattle bones inscribed when the Chinese writing system was being developed 1400 or 1500 years prior to Liu Shang's time – maybe even earlier.

What interested Liu Shang was not so much the content of the writings as the characters themselves. Hieroglyphics had been developed into a highly complex and sophisticated system of tens of thousands of characters.

Some characters are simple enough for even a child to decipher. One, two, and three are, respectively, simply one, two and three horizontal strokes increasing in size. 'Man' is a simple stick figure with no arms and two legs. The character for 'person' is in the shape of an open mouth. To the educated classes, a person is the only living creature capable of speech. To the poor, a person is another mouth to feed!

Most characters tell a story. The character for peace is the character for woman under the character for roof. The character for quarrel is *two* characters for woman under the character for roof!

Liu Shang could easily understand those characters, but other characters puzzled him. Why was the character for 'boat' made up of the radicals 'vessel + eight + people'? Why was the character meaning 'to create' made up of the radicals for 'speak + dust + life + walk'? Why was the character meaning 'to covet or desire' made from 'two trees + woman'? Why was the character meaning 'forbidden or to warn' made from 'two trees + God'? Why did the radicals 'dust + breath + two persons' all within the radical for 'enclosure' make up the character for 'garden'? What stories had prompted the creation of these characters?

When Liu Shang could find no answers to these questions in the literature to which he had access, he asked the astrologers and wise men in the emperor's court. None of them could answer his questions. That is when Liu Shang decided to act upon the idea he had gotten from his grandfather. He would travel west along the Silk Road and confer with wise men in other countries. Maybe the truth had originated outside China.

Liu Shang hired some servants to travel with him and loaded several camels with personal belongings, stargazing equipment, food and plenty of silk to finance his journey. He expected his search for truth to take him away from home for several years. He would also have to learn new languages.

At every major city along the Silk Road, Liu Shang sought out the local community of magi. To his disappointment, most of them appeared to be sorcerers enjoying the wealth and life style afforded by their occupation rather than being wise men seeking the truth. Some of them laughed at Liu Shang for being so naive as to think that there was such a thing as absolute truth.

Finally in India Liu Shang found a kindred spirit by the name of Balthazar. When he consulted the stars, it was not a matter of hocus-pocus or show, as so many magi did with a wink. He actually believed the stars had something to say, and tried to hear what they were saying. Mostly he came away from a time of quiet listening with a deep sense of awe and wonder.

Both men agreed that the truth was likely to be found in one supreme god rather than in a pantheon of many gods. Even if there were many gods, surely only the greatest of them would be worthy of worship! Balthazar had never heard of ShangDi, but he knew that Zoroastrians believed in one god. That religion or philosophy had originated in Persia. Maybe there they would find the truth.

They decided to continue westward toward Persia. Liu Shang was happy for the company of someone other than his servants.

3 BC

In Susa, the capital of Persia, Liu Shang and Balthazar soon found a community of magi, all of whom were eager to discuss and compare ideas. But the 'truths' they espoused did not ring true with the two men.

"How will we recognize the truth when we see it?" Balthazar asked Liu Shang. "How will we know when a so-called wise man is speaking truth and not just blowing smoke in our eyes?"

"I've been thinking about that," said Liu Shang. "I think the true wise man will already have said something unusual which is verifiably true. Then we will be able to trust him for what is not yet verified."

One day Liu Shang and Balthazar met two magi who seemed different from the rest. Caspar and Melchior, like Liu Shang and Balthazar, were foreigners in Persia.

Caspar was from Arabia, though his ancestors were from northern Africa. Caspar had spent years in Babylon learning from the magi there, but was not satisfied that he had yet found the truth.

Melchior, a Chaldee, was a Jew from Yemen. Melchior was well educated in languages, priestly rituals and astrology, but he had come to Persia to study other philosophies. He soon became disillusioned by the magi in Persia. Somehow their teachings did not ring true, and their lives were not consistent with their expressed beliefs. So he had decided to explore more fully his roots – the Hebrew Scriptures. The only Hebrew book he had brought with him to Persia was the book of Daniel, a text known to all magi in Babylon and Susa.

When Melchior learned that Liu Shang and Balthazar were looking for a wise man who was believable, Melchior said, "I think I have discovered the man you are looking for. Caspar and I have been studying the writings of Daniel, a member of the Jewish nobility who was deported to Babylon by King Nebuchadnezzar following the siege of Jerusalem 600 years ago."

Liu Shang and Balthazar expressed interest in joining Melchior and Caspar in their study of Daniel's writings, but only if they could be convinced that Daniel was a wise man they could trust to tell the truth. When Liu Shang and Balthazar enquired as to Daniel's credentials, Melchior gave them a short history lesson.

"In the second year of King Nebuchadnezzar's reign," he told them, "the king had a dream which troubled him so much that he couldn't sleep, so he summoned the magicians, enchanters, sorcerers and astrologers. He asked them not just to interpret his dream, but to tell him what he had dreamed! The magi objected that the king was asking the impossible. Nevertheless, Nebuchadnezzar continued to insist that they tell him the dream first. Any fool with an imagination can interpret a dream, the king reasoned. But if someone could tell him his dream, he would know that the interpretation – the easy part – was reliable."

Liu Shang nodded his approval. "I like the king's logic."

Melchior continued with his story. "When the magi could not tell the king his dream, he ordered them executed. As a result, the commander of the king's guard arrested Daniel, who was one of the king's wise men. Upon learning of the king's harsh decree, Daniel asked for time to ask his God about the dream. Not long afterward, Daniel was able to tell the king his dream and the magi were spared execution. To this day Daniel is highly respected throughout Babylonia and Persia."

"What was the dream?" asked Balthazar.

"Nebuchadnezzar had dreamed about an enormous, dazzling statue with a gold head, silver chest and arms, bronze belly and thighs, iron legs and feet of iron mixed with clay. Daniel explained that the statue represented a series of world governments, starting with the Babylonian empire. Nebuchadnezzar was the head of gold. The other kingdoms were in the future, and Daniel proceeded to foretell what was to come. Nebuchadnezzar concluded that Daniel's God was the God of gods, the Lord of kings and the revealer of mysteries."

"I would conclude the same," said Liu Shang.

"But knowing that did not produce a change in Nebuchadnezzar's behavior," Melchior noted. "Some time later, he had another dream which none of his magi could interpret. By this time the king, recognizing that the spirit of the holy gods was in Daniel, had promoted him to chief of the magicians. Daniel was reluctant to tell the king the interpretation of this dream because it was not good news. The dream foretold that Nebuchadnezzar would go mad, have his royal authority taken away, and be driven out of the palace to live with the wild animals and eat grass like cattle. Seven years would pass with him in that condition, Daniel warned, unless the king repented of his wickedness and acknowledged the sovereignty of the Most High God.

"Twelve months later Daniel's prophecy came to pass. Nebuchadnezzar was walking on the roof of his royal palace in Babylon. As his heart swelled with pride, he boasted, 'Is not this the great Babylon I have built by my mighty power and for the glory of my majesty?'

"Boom! The words were still on his lips when a voice spoke from heaven and everything Daniel prophesied came true. Nebuchadnezzar went crazy and lived and behaved like a wild animal. At the end of seven years, his sanity was restored as predicted. Nebuchadnezzar quickly praised the Most High God before another calamity should befall him. He said, 'Now I, Nebuchadnezzar, praise and exalt and glorify the King of heaven, because everything he does is right and all his ways are just. And those who walk in pride he is able to humble.'"

Liu Shang gasped. "That prayer is so similar to Emperor Ai's prayer to ShangDi during the Border Sacrifice! It's amazing!" he exclaimed. "Even the name ShangDi means the same – the Ruler Above, or God Most High. Emperor Ai expressed a humility I knew he didn't feel, but he must have been praying to the same God as Nebuchadnezzar prayed to!"

Sensing that Balthazar was still somewhat skeptical, Melchior continued to give examples of prophesies of Daniel which had come true.

"Daniel lived a long time and remained in the royal court through the reigns of several kings in Babylon," Melchior said. "King Belshazzar, like his father Nebuchadnezzar before him, did not humble himself before the Most High God. Belshazzar had not learned from his father's seven years of humiliation. During a great banquet that he hosted for a thousand of his nobles, suddenly the fingers of a human hand appeared and wrote mysteriously on the wall in the royal palace. Again the king called for the enchanters, astrologers and diviners to interpret the writing, and none was able to do so."But the queen mother remembered Daniel. She said to the king, 'Don't be alarmed! There is a man in your kingdom who has the spirit of the holy gods in him. Call for Daniel, and he will tell you what the writing means.'

"Daniel interpreted the writing, but it was bad news for Belshazzar: 'God has numbered the days of your reign and brought it to an end. You have been weighed on the scales and found wanting. Your kingdom is divided and given to the Medes and Persians.' That very night Daniel's prophecy came true. Belshazzar, king of the Babylonians, was killed, and Darius the Mede took over the kingdom.

"King Darius, like his predecessors, soon learned the power of Daniel's God. Daniel so distinguished himself by his exceptional qualities that King Darius planned to set him over the whole kingdom. The administrators who had been bypassed for promotion were so jealous that they devised a plot to get rid of Daniel. They tricked the king into decreeing that for thirty days no one should pray to any god other than King Darius himself. The penalty for breaking this law was to be thrown into the lions' den.

"The administrators knew that Daniel was in the habit, three times a day, of retreating to his home, opening his upstairs windows toward Jerusalem, and kneeling to pray to his God. When Daniel, fully aware of the king's decree, continued to pray three times a day to God Most High, the administrators gleefully reported him to the king. King Darius tried to circumvent the law, but his administrators would not let him. Reluctantly the king gave the order, and Daniel was thrown into the lions' den.

"Then the most amazing thing happened – the lions didn't touch Daniel! At the first light of dawn, the king hurried to the lions' den, hoping against hope that Daniel was still alive. In an anguished voice he called out, 'Daniel, servant of the living God, has your God, whom you serve continually, been able to rescue you from the lions?'

"Daniel answered, 'O king, live forever! My God sent his angel, and he shut the mouths of the lions. They have not hurt me, because I was found innocent in his sight.'

"No sooner was Daniel lifted out, without a scratch on him, than the king ordered all of Daniel's accusers, along with their wives and children, thrown to the lions. The lions killed them before they touched the floor of the den."

"Served them right!" exclaimed Balthazar, who had been totally captivated by the story.

Melchior concluded his story: "During the rest of Darius' reign, all of the subjects in his kingdom were ordered to fear and reverence the God of Daniel."

There was silence for a few moments. Finally Liu Shang spoke up. "Maybe we, too, should worship the God of Daniel."

"I agree," said Balthazar. "But how do we do that?"

"Let's do it the way Daniel did," suggested Caspar. "He gave thanks to his God and asked Him for help." Quietly the four men thanked God Most High for bringing them together, and asked Him to help them in their search for truth.

Liu Shang and his friends began to read and re-read the book of Daniel. As they did so, they became more firmly convinced that Daniel's God was the true God and Daniel was his messenger. They resolved to follow Daniel's example to the best of their ability. Maybe the secret to hearing from God was to be found in Daniel's rituals. Whenever it was practical, they lived on Daniel's diet of vegetables and water. They also followed Daniel's pattern of praying. Three times a day they went to an upstairs room where the windows faced Jerusalem. There they opened the windows, then got down on their knees and prayed, giving thanks to God Most High and asking Him for help.

Soon the four came to understand that some of Daniel's prophecies had already been fulfilled, either in Daniel's lifetime or in the five or six hundred years since. Some prophecies appeared to refer to a time in the distant future, a time Daniel referred to as "the end." Some prophecies were interpreted by God to Daniel, while others were inscrutable.

Then Caspar noticed one prophecy which appeared to be imminent. Caspar read from the book of Daniel: "'Seventy sevens are decreed for your people and your holy city....'"

"He's talking about the Jewish people and Jerusalem," Melchior explained.

Caspar continued reading. "'Know and understand this.'"

"Good!" exclaimed Melchior in relief. "This isn't one of those visions that Daniel saw but didn't understand."

Caspar patiently endured the interruptions. "'From the issuing of the decree to restore and rebuild Jerusalem until the Anointed One, the ruler, comes, there will be seven sevens, and sixty-two sevens. It will be rebuilt with streets and a trench, but in times of trouble. After the sixty-two sevens, the Anointed One will be cut off and will have nothing.'[7] Then the passage talks about what will happen in 'the end,'" Caspar said, "which is not of immediate interest to us."

"What are 'sevens'?" asked Liu Shang.

Melchior, with his background in Jewish culture and history, knew the answer. "That's easy. Every Jew knows the answer. 'Sevens' are weeks of years. Every seventh year the Jews, by law, are required to give their land a rest."

But Melchior's thoughts were on a different part of the reading from Daniel.

"'Know and understand...,'" Melchior repeated thoughtfully. "I know and understand when the time frame of that prophecy begins. It begins with the decree issued by Artaxerxes Longimanus, king of Persia, to restore and rebuild Jerusalem. His decree provided his cupbearer, Nehemiah, with safe-conduct from the palace right here in Susa to Jerusalem and appointed him as governor to oversee the restoration. Artaxerxes even provided timber from his royal forest for the rebuilding. I also 'know and understand' that the builders faced strong opposition – 'trouble', as Daniel described it – yet they completed the task exactly 49 years later – seven sevens – just as Daniel foretold."

"But what's this about an 'anointed one'?" Balthazar asked.

"Jewish kings were anointed by the high priest in recognition that they were chosen by God," explained Melchior. "King David often referred to himself in his prayers to God as 'your anointed one,' but Jews also believe in a greater Anointed One who is still to come. The Hebrew word for Anointed One is Messiah. He will be no ordinary king, but the King of kings."

"And this Anointed One will come as ruler at the end of 'seven sevens and sixty-two sevens'," Liu Shang remarked.

Caspar began busily scribbling numbers on a piece of papyrus.

"What are you doing?" asked Liu Shang.

"I'm calculating," Caspar said. "Seven sevens and 62 sevens are 69 sevens, or 483 years. If the sevens started with the decree to rebuild Jerusalem, then we are about 33 years from the time the Anointed One comes as ruler."

"That means he is either alive today or soon to be born," reasoned Balthazar.

"I don't think he has been born yet," said Liu Shang.

"How can you be so sure?" asked Caspar.

"The thought just struck me. I think if this Anointed One is anointed by ShangDi, who created heaven and earth, he would announce it," declared Liu Shang.

"How?" asked Balthazar.

"I'm not sure," said Liu Shang slowly, "but it would have to be in a language everyone could understand. After all, ShangDi, who made the earth, would want all its inhabitants to know about such an auspicious birth, don't you think?"

"I wish I had brought more Hebrew Scriptures with me," said Melchior. "I know the Jewish prophets had lots to say about the Anointed One, our Messiah. But when I left my home in Yemen, I didn't realize that the truth I was seeking was right under my nose. I just didn't pay much attention to the idea of a Messiah. He had been so long in coming that I wasn't expecting him to come in my lifetime. He didn't seem relevant to me. Let's just say his star wasn't on my horizon."

"Don't feel badly," said Caspar. "Didn't Liu Shang just say that God Most High would speak in a language everyone would understand? Not very many people outside of Judea and a few Jewish communities scattered throughout the Arab world can speak or read Hebrew."

"Most of the eastern world, thanks to the Han dynasty, speaks Chinese; and most of the western world, thanks to

Alexander the Great, speaks Greek," said Balthazar. "The rest speak in a thousand different tongues. There is no universal language understood by all."

"And even the languages we do speak are not fully understood by their speakers," said Liu Shang.

"What do you mean?" asked Caspar.

"I was thinking of my own Chinese language," said Liu Shang. "I don't understand the derivation of many of our Chinese characters. For instance, why is our character for 'boat' made up of the radicals 'vessel + eight + people'?"

"I know," said Melchior.

Liu Shang looked at him in surprise.

"Our Hebrew Scriptures tell the story, which could easily be summed up in that one character. The boat is Noah's ark, and the eight people are Noah and his wife, and his three sons and their wives."

"Not so fast!" said Liu Shang. "Who is Noah? And what is this about an ark?"

Melchior then told the story. "Long, long ago, God saw the wickedness of mankind and decided to wipe out the whole earth with a flood. He chose to start afresh with Noah, the most righteous man on earth. God instructed Noah to build an ark to save his family of eight and two of each animal species. Anybody who wished could join Noah on the ark, but nobody did. They didn't believe God would do such a thing. When the Chinese written language was being developed, your people must have known this story."

"That's just one character," argued Liu Shang. "It must be a coincidence that your story fits. What about the character for 'to create'? Why is it made up of the radicals for 'speak + dust or mud + life + walk'?"

Melchior had the answer for that one, too. "All creation was spoken into existence by God. After creating everything except mankind, God said, 'Let's make man in our image.' Then he formed man out of dust, breathed life into him and he walked and talked. Your character for 'create' explains how God created man."

"What about the character for garden – 'dust + breath + two persons' all within the radical for 'enclosure'?"

Again Melchior had a story to fit. "The two persons are Adam and Eve. God created the first man, Adam, by breathing into a creature sculpted from the dust. Then he made a woman, whom Adam named Eve. God gave them a special place to live. He put them both into a beautiful enclosed garden."

The answers to Liu Shang's questions were coming so fast that he decided to ask a few more.

"And the character meaning 'forbidden or to warn'? Why is it made from 'two trees + God'?"

"In the garden Adam and Eve had everything they could possibly need or want. But there were two special trees. One was the Tree of Life. Whoever ate of it would live forever. The other was the Tree of the Knowledge of Good and Evil. Adam and Eve were forbidden to eat from it. God warned them, 'When you eat of it you will surely die.'"

"How could the knowledge of good and evil kill them?" asked Liu Shang skeptically.

"It wasn't the tree itself that was dangerous," explained Melchior. "The tree was a test to see if Adam and Eve would obey God. Nothing in the whole garden was off limits except that one tree."

"I think I can guess the answer to my next question," said Liu Shang. "The character meaning 'to covet or desire' is made from 'two trees + woman'. I guess the woman coveted the fruit of the two special trees."

"Close," smiled Melchior. "God didn't tell Adam and Eve about the Tree of Life. If he did, surprisingly they didn't covet the fruit of it. But Eve did covet the fruit of the Tree of the Knowledge of Good and Evil. She ate of it and then gave some to Adam. God had to drive them both out of the garden before they could eat of the Tree of Life and live forever. That's where the second tree came into the story."

"So they didn't fall down dead?" asked Liu Shang.

"No, but something died inside, and they died eventually," said Melchior. "Now all mankind suffers the same fate."

"What about our character for 'come'?" ask Liu Shang. "A cross with three people on it – one large person in the middle and two smaller ones on either side? A cross is the sign for ten, and according to Chinese tradition, ten represents completion. How could those concepts possibly add up to 'come'?"

Melchior didn't have an answer. He could think of no story in the Hebrew Scriptures that explained that Chinese character.

"Maybe that is like our Chinese concept of yin yang," Liu Shang concluded, thinking out loud. "Complementary opposites within a greater whole. Seemingly contrary forces which are interconnected and interdependent in the natural world. Maybe the character for 'come' is just a paradox we have to live with."

Liu Shang could have asked about many other Chinese characters, but he decided to leave them for a later time.

"Enough about your language, Liu Shang," said Balthazar. "We are looking for a universal language that God Most High could use to announce his Anointed One."

"I know what it is," said Caspar.

His three friends looked at him in surprise.

"It's right under our noses. Maybe I should say it's over our heads! The language that brought all of us together. The language of the stars!"

"Explain," requested Liu Shang.

"We are magi. We study the stars. Anybody who studies the heavens must know that there is a great God who created this universe," Caspar explained patiently. "Those who don't

see it are blind. Maybe even deaf. If God Most High has anything important to say, he will say it through something the
whole world can see – through the stars."

"I see," said Liu Shang. "Like a comet, or an eclipse, or
an alignment of planets foretelling the birth or death of an
emperor."

"Yes," said Melchior. "We must watch the skies diligently until God speaks."

"It should be soon," added Balthazar.

"We must continue to pray to ShangDi and ask Him to
help us read the heavens and understand correctly what He
is saying to us," said Liu Shang.

The four men set up a schedule for watching the night
sky. They would each take a three-hour shift on clear nights,
which in the desert was almost every night.

During the day they continued to study the writings of
Daniel, and they speculated as to what form God's voice
would take. They discussed whether a comet, an eclipse of
the sun or moon, or an alignment of planets would be a sign.

"Comets often herald the births and deaths of princes,"
said Melchior. "One appeared at Julius Caesar's death forty
years ago."

"I saw a comet the last year I was in China," said Liu
Shang. "Our lamentable emperor didn't die, though some
wished he would."

"Two years ago Mars, Jupiter and Saturn were aligned
in the constellation Pisces," said Caspar. "The Romans con-
sider Jupiter to be the king of planets. Maybe that alignment signified something about royalty and we missed its
significance."

"Two months later the sun, Jupiter, the moon and Saturn
all aligned in the constellation Aries while Venus and Mars
were in neighboring constellations," said Balthazar. "That
was even more auspicious. Most of the Zoroastrian astrolo-

gers I talked to believed the planetary alignment in Aries was a sign a powerful leader was born."

"Speaking of alignments in the heavens," said Liu Shang, "for the next three weeks the sun will be aligned between the shoulders and knees of the woman in the constellation Virgo."

"That could highlight a pregnancy and signify a royal birth," commented Balthazar.

"Or it could signify nothing," said Caspar. "This alignment happens every year at this time. We will have to watch carefully over the next few days to see if anything else happens."

"According to the Hebrew Zodiac," said Melchior, "the constellation Virgo, in the time of King David, denoted Ruth gleaning in the fields of Boaz. Since Isaiah's prophecy in the time of King Hezekiah, Virgo has denoted the Virgin who will give birth to a son called Immanuel, which means 'God with us.' Isaiah prophesied, 'For to us a child is born, to us a son is given, and the government will be on his shoulders. And he will be called Wonderful Counselor, Mighty God, Everlasting Father, Prince of Peace.... He will reign on David's throne and over his kingdom, establishing and upholding it with justice and righteousness from that time on and forever.'"[8]

"Most of the astrologers in this part of the world recognize the sign of Virgo as the sign under which a messianic world ruler will be born from a virgin,"[9] agreed Caspar. "The brightest star in the constellation is Spica, in the virgin's left hand. Spica in Arabic means 'the branch',[10] but I don't know if that has any significance."

During the next few nights, the four men watched the night sky with a heightened sense of expectation. Then one evening as the sun was setting, Liu Shang spotted a bright star just above the horizon. At first he thought it was Venus, the brightest object in the sky other than the sun and moon.

But it wasn't where Venus should be. Turning, he saw Venus in its usual place. Liu Shang ran to call his friends, who began to dance with glee.

"The timing is perfect!" exclaimed Melchior. "Sundown today is the beginning of Rosh Hashanah, the perfect time for a Jewish king to be born!"

Melchior's friends were not familiar with Jewish culture, so he elaborated. "Our religious year begins with the first new moon in spring, but our civic year begins in the fall, six months later. Rosh Hashanah is our New Year's Day for governmental affairs. Jewish kings count their years of reign from that day, whether or not that was the day they were crowned. If a king was crowned on any day other than Rosh Hashanah, the time from his coronation to Rosh Hashanah would be considered the first year of his reign. His second year of reign would begin on the first New Year's Day following his coronation, even if he had been king for only a week. Many historians have been confused by the way we keep record of our kings."

Their excitement soon drew the attention of others nearby. But they couldn't see what the four Magi were excited about.

"Look!" said Liu Shang, pointing to the star. "Look at that bright star. It's new!"

They stared for a while in the direction Liu Shang was pointing, then looked toward him as if he were crazy.

"There's nothing bright in that direction. Just a million faint stars."

"No, the bright one! Brighter than Venus!" said Balthazar, joining Liu Shang, Caspar and Melchior as they pointed. But the others shook their heads.

The four friends looked at each other in bewilderment as the crowd drifted away. Nobody else could see the star! Were they hallucinating? they wondered. All four were awake all night. They could see the star plainly until sunrise.

41

After a fitful sleep, the four again met to discuss what they had seen the night before. They prayed fervently to God Most High to help them understand what had happened. At sunset the star appeared again, but nobody else could see what they were seeing.

"Have we gone mad?" Balthazar asked, expressing what the others were thinking. "Have we so focused on the Anointed One prophesied by Daniel that we have convinced ourselves of something that is not there? What is truth and what is fiction?"

The four searched the royal libraries for anything that might solve the mystery. Finally they discovered copies of the Hebrew historical Scriptures. Of particular interest were the five books of Moses and the book of Samuel-Kings.

Caspar came across the story of Elisha at a time when the king of Aram was at war with Israel.

When every military move of the Arameans was known to the king of Israel in advance, the king of Aram suspected a spy in his midst. He was told that Elisha the prophet was telling the king of Israel the very words the king of Aram spoke in his bedroom. So the king of Aram sent his army in full force to surround the city in which Elisha lived and capture him. Elisha's servant got up one morning and was dismayed to see the Aramean army with horses and chariots surrounding the city.

Panicking, the servant asked his master, "What shall we do?"

"Don't be afraid," the prophet answered. "Those who are with us are more than those who are with them."

When Elisha prayed that the Lord would open his servant's eyes, the Lord answered and he saw what Elisha was seeing – the hills all around them were full of horses and chariots of fire!

"Do you think that is what has happened to us?" Caspar asked his friends. "Do you think God Most High has opened our eyes to see what others cannot see?"

"You mean we are not hallucinating?" asked Liu Shang. "The star is really there, but others are blind to it?"

"It makes sense to me," said Balthazar. "We have been praying to God to help us."

"Then we must be seeing the sign of the Anointed One, our Messiah," concluded Melchior. "He must be born!"

"We must go see him!" exclaimed Balthazar.

"Not so fast," cautioned Liu Shang. "Judea is a long way away. It will take weeks to prepare for the journey and months to get there. What if we are wrong?"

They decided to wait for further confirmation that they had come to the right conclusion. Again the four searched through their books. They quickly gave up asking advice from other magi, who couldn't see what Liu Shang and his friends continued to see in the night sky.

One day while Liu Shang was reading, he gave a shout of triumph. "I found it!" he told his friends.

"Found what?" asked Caspar.

"Found the confirmation that we are on the right track," responded Liu Shang. "Look here in the fourth book of Moses. A sorcerer named Balaam uttered an oracle: 'A *star* will come out of Jacob; a scepter will rise out of Israel.' He foretold that the sign of a special king would be a star! We have seen that star – his star!"

"I remember the story of Balaam," said Melchior, "but I had forgotten exactly what he said. I remembered only that he blessed Israel instead of cursing them as the king of Moab requested."

The four immediately began preparations for their journey to Israel. They weren't sure exactly where in Israel, but quickly concluded that a king would be born in the palace in the capital city of Jerusalem. At night they continued to observe the special star.

"Last night the star seemed to be beckoning to me," said Liu Shang to his friends one morning. "Am I going crazy?"

"I, too, have experienced that," said Balthazar, "but I didn't worry that I was going crazy. I have always believed that the stars have something to say to us. In recent nights I felt I was on the verge of actually hearing what the special star was saying. I can imagine it saying, 'Come. Follow me.' It makes me want to hurry, finish our preparations, and start the journey."

Soon the discussion turned to what gifts to bring to the newborn king. All four men were wealthy, and they pooled their resources. Liu Shang had silk, one of China's most prized exports. Caspar and Melchior had valuable spices, frankincense and myrrh. Balthazar's wealth was mainly in gold from Ophir in India, though he, too, had some frankincense.

The men wanted to bring not only gifts of value, but gifts of significance. Gold, they all agreed, was the perfect gift for a king. It symbolized royalty. Silk they weren't so sure about; but it was great as currency to purchase other things of value. Both frankincense and myrrh were expensive and were prized as ingredients in perfume, sacred anointing oil, cosmetic products and embalming spices. Many magi used the spices for their priestly duties in their places of worship.

As the four made preparations for their journey, they continued to study Hebrew Scriptures and observe the heavens. One day Liu Shang's friends found him reading with a concerned look on his face.

"What's the matter?" asked Balthazar.

"I've been rereading Daniel – that passage about the Anointed One," replied Liu Shang. "It says, 'After the sixty-two sevens, the Anointed One will be cut off and will have nothing.' Doesn't that mean that he will be killed?"

"It sure sounds like it," said Balthazar.

For a while the four men debated amongst themselves how that could be. If he was King of kings and anointed by God Most High, surely no one could harm him. They were still discussing the issue when Balthazar reminded his friends that it was time for prayer. They asked God for help in understanding the things the angel had told Daniel to know and understand.

After the prayer session, Melchior spoke up. "I have vague recollections that some of our prophets said things that could be interpreted to mean the Messiah would be killed, but most of our people dismiss such an idea. We want someone who will deliver us from our miseries and from our oppressors."

"At the end of his book, Daniel said, 'None of the wicked will understand, but those who are wise will understand,'"[11] remembered Caspar. "We must study to see what the holy books say, and not read our wishes into them."

"I don't wish this to be true," said Liu Shang solemnly, "but Daniel seems to indicate that the Anointed One will be both crowned as ruler and cut off in a short period of time – possibly within the same year."

"If that is so," commented Caspar, "our gifts are even more appropriate. Frankincense and myrrh, for all their other potential uses, are also valued for embalming the dead."

near Jerusalem
December, 2 BC

The four Magi grew more excited as they approached Jerusalem. All four had experienced the sensation that the star was beckoning to them. They followed it eagerly. The four had also experienced a growing sense of awe and wonder as they followed it.

"What a king he must be," exclaimed Liu Shang, "to have such a star to announce his birth!"

"And to be prophesied about so long ago!" Caspar added. "Daniel wrote more than 500 years ago about the Anointed One who would be revealed after 69 sevens, and Balaam prophesied 1400 years ago about his star!"

"Tomorrow we will be in Jerusalem and we will finally see him," said Melchior. "I doubt we will get much sleep tonight."

Melchior was right about the sleep, but not for the reason he expected. They camped just outside Jerusalem, planning to enter the city as soon as the sun rose. The night was clear, but the star was nowhere to be seen.

"I can't see the star!" Balthazar said in dismay to no one in particular. His servants didn't react. They could see lots of stars, but nothing unusual. The servants had never seen the star that the Magi made so much fuss about.

"I can't see the star!" Balthazar said again, this time to his three friends. None of them could see the star! They slept fitfully that night, getting up frequently to check the sky, only to be disappointed.

They got up at early light and were the first ones at the city gates. Impatiently they waited for the gates to be opened. Once inside, they asked a question they expected anyone in the street would be able to answer: "Where is the one who has been born king of the Jews? We saw his star in the east and have come to worship him."

The question caused quite a stir in the streets. To say the citizens of Jerusalem were troubled would be to put it mildly. Some were frightened, even terrified. They had seen what their paranoid king had done before when he felt his throne threatened. King Herod had already executed two of his sons because he feared they were conspiring to take his throne. A third son was under suspicion, but so far had escaped execution. Word in the streets was that the Roman emperor Caesar Augustus had joked, "I'd rather be Herod's sow than Herod's son." The joke was that Herod, being a Jew, didn't eat pigs, but he murdered his sons!

It didn't take long for word to reach the palace that an elaborate entourage from the East was in Jerusalem inquiring about the birth of the "King of the Jews." Herod was deeply troubled at this new threat to his throne, but he did his best to hide his feelings.

He invited the Magi into his court and entertained them with excessive politeness. They repeated their question. "Where is the one who has been born king of the Jews? We saw his star in the east and have come to worship him."

Nobody in Herod's court had heard of an unusual star, but Herod took the Magi's quest seriously. He understood immediately that this child they sought was no normal king, but the Messiah himself. What neither Herod nor the Magi knew was where the king was to be born. Magnanimously, Herod offered to help the Magi in their quest by calling together all the people's chief priests and teachers of the law and asking them where the Messiah was to be born.

They soon had the answer. "In Bethlehem in Judea," they replied, quoting the prophet Micah. "'But you, Bethlehem, in the land of Judah, are by no means least among the rulers of Judah; for out of you will come a ruler who will be the shepherd of my people Israel.'"[12]

The chief priests and rabbis were careful to treat King Herod respectfully – he had been known to execute rabbis who displeased him – but they did not take the Magi seriously. The chief priests were part time astrologers of sorts, as the annual Jewish feasts were determined by phases of the moon. But the priests had seen no unusual star announcing Messiah's birth. If the Messiah had been born, they would be the first to know. After all, they were the spiritual leaders of Israel and the keepers of truth.

Out of earshot of the Magi, the priests and rabbis secretly made fun of the Magi's claim that a king of the Jews had been born. One of the priests recalled some shepherds who claimed that the Messiah had been born the previous year during a Roman census.

"They claimed the Messiah had been born in a stable," he laughed. "Born to a poor carpenter and his wife from Nazareth! So poor they couldn't afford a room in the inn! You can be sure the true Messiah's arrival will be nothing like that!"

"Aha!" exclaimed another, joining in the fun. "But he *was* born in Bethlehem!"

"Yes, but born to a little whore who got pregnant before she was married!" sneered another. "She had the audacity to claim to be a virgin even though the presence of a baby proved otherwise!"

"The prophet Isaiah did say that Immanuel would be born to a virgin," declared one rabbi weakly, but his words were ignored as the conversation deteriorated into course jokes.

Herod dismissed the priests and rabbis, but he did not dismiss the idea that the Magi had seen something no one else had seen. If Old Testament prophets heard from God when others heard nothing, why was it so strange to think that Magi – the counterpart of prophets in Gentile cultures – could see what others did not? Herod did not believe that Jewish priests and rabbis were the exclusive custodians of truth.

Herod secretly interrogated the Magi to find out the exact time the star had appeared. Their answer he found alarming. The star had appeared on Rosh Hashanah a year and three months earlier. Rosh Hashanah was the date from which Jewish kings measured their reign! The timing had to be significant.

Hiding his alarm, Herod sent the Magi to Bethlehem, saying, "Go and make a careful search for the child. As soon as you find him, report to me, so that I too may go and worship him."

Herod claimed to want to worship the newborn Messiah, but his real desire was far more sinister. Herod wasn't a descendent of David. He reigned as king of the Jews by appointment from Rome. If a descendent of David were to rise, Herod's reign and that of his descendents would be over. Messiah or not, this child must be destroyed.

The Magi were blissfully unaware of King Herod's motives. They were simply happy to be once again on their way to visit the newborn king. The events at the palace had taken up most of the day, which was short this time of year. They were half way on their two hour journey from Jerusalem to Bethlehem when the sun set. Fortunately, a full moon was rising, enabling them to continue in the bright moonlight.

Suddenly Liu Shang pointed straight ahead and cried out, "Look!"

There in front of them was the star they had seen in the east and followed all the way to Judea. Their servants watched in amusement as the Magi dismounted from their camels, threw their dignity to the stars and danced for joy. They slapped each other on the back, hugged each other, laughed and cried, then danced again.

As they looked at the star, it seemed to beckon to them. The Magi mounted their camels as quickly as they could to follow it. Immediately the star zoomed toward them.

As the Magi followed, the star went ahead of them, maintaining a constant distance until they reached the village of Bethlehem. Then the star drew closer still, leading them through the winding streets until it stopped directly over a small ordinary-looking house.

The Magi waited for a few moments to be sure the star had really stopped. The house was neat and tidy, but so tiny that it obviously belonged to a poor man. Could this be the right place? The home of a king? The star settled a little lower in the sky until it seemed to almost touch the roof.

"This must be the place," Liu Shang concluded.

While the Magi were dismounting, a man came out of the little house to investigate the caravan of exotic travelers who had stopped in front of his humble home.

"Where is the one who has been born king of the Jews?" Melchior asked for the third time that day. "We saw his star in the east and have come to worship him."

"Mary!" the man called to his wife. "We have visitors!"

Joseph introduced himself to the strangely dressed men as Mary scurried around to straighten up the house. Liu Shang, Balthazar, Caspar and Melchior were impatient to meet the child. Eagerly they entered the house.

As Mary lifted the toddler from his little crib, Balthazar asked, "What is his name?"

"Jesus," answered Mary softly, her voice warm with love and pride.

"His name means 'savior'," explained Joseph, "because he will save his people from their sins. That's what an angel told me in a dream. The angel also said, 'They will call him Immanuel, which means, God with us.'"

It was good to be able to speak openly about the child to people who didn't scoff, thought Joseph.

One by one the richly dressed Magi bowed low before the child, taking turns to speak quietly to him in worship. When Caspar clapped his hands, servants approached, carrying gifts. The Magi took the gifts and held them toward the child.

Mary set little Jesus on the floor and the Magi soon squatted in a circle facing him. One by one they presented their gifts, letting Jesus open them, helping him when his tiny hands couldn't manage. As the lids of the treasure chests were lifted, the glitter of gold and the aroma of precious spices filled the room. Little Jesus babbled and smiled, then toddled around to kiss and hug each of the Magi, who kissed and hugged him back. The Magi were sure Jesus understood what was happening. They were convinced – rightly – that they were in the presence of the Messiah, the King of the Jews.

Mary and Joseph were awestruck. Nothing this amazing had happened since the night Jesus was born, when shepherds found them in the stable behind the inn. The shepherds had told tales of an angel announcing the birth and a host of angels singing, "Glory to God in the highest, and on earth peace among men of goodwill." It was because the angel had said they would find the baby in a manger that the shepherds had thought to look in the stable.

This evening would be like that night over a year ago – an experience to treasure and ponder for years to come. Gold. Frankincense. Myrrh. Gifts fit for a king! What did it all mean?

Mary didn't have time to figure it all out. Her little one was tired, and she needed to put him to bed. Afterwards, Joseph and Mary visited with the Magi long into the night.

When they finally left, none of them slept well. Liu Shang, Balthazar, Caspar and Melchior woke to discover they had all dreamed the same dream. Herod, current king of the Jews, had no intention of worshiping the future King of the Jews. Herod saw the child as a threat to his dynasty. He intended to kill him. The Magi returned to their country by another route, entirely bypassing the palace.

On their return trip the Magi had plenty to talk about. Little Jesus had shattered all their preconceived notions of what an earthly king would be like. He was not rich; in fact, he could hardly be poorer. He was not born to noble parents, yet he was a descendant of King David, and God Most High was his father. His birth had not been announced with trumpets as a newborn king usually was, yet it had been announced by a whole choir of angels – to a few humble shepherds!

Little Jesus also shattered the preconceived notions of the Jewish religious leaders, the very ones who claimed to be looking for the Anointed One. The chief priests and teachers of the Law who had been called to the palace by King Herod didn't even bother to investigate what the Magi were looking into. They had heard the stories the shepherds told and not even traveled the five miles to Bethlehem to explore the possibility that the Messiah was born.

This king with such an unconventional start in life must be destined for an unconventional finish, concluded the Magi. They would love to return when the child became king, but would probably be too old by then – if they were still alive. They would have to content themselves with researching the entire Hebrew Scriptures, especially the prophets, to learn more about this King who embodied truth.

What had one prophet called him? Immanuel – God with us. What a name! What a concept! That the Creator would come to earth to live amongst his creation! To demonstrate what God is like!

"That beats listening to the stars," said Balthazar. "What questions I would love to ask him! God in human form!"

Back in Bethlehem the night of the Magi's visit, Joseph, too, had a dream. In it an angel told him to escape to Egypt because Herod wanted to kill the child. The angel would tell them when it was safe to return. Without waiting for sunrise,

Joseph awakened Mary, quickly packed whatever they could carry and left Bethlehem for Egypt. The gifts of the Magi would go a long way toward providing for their family of three in Egypt.

Joseph and Mary had lots to talk about on their journey to Egypt. Uppermost in their minds were the events of their last night in Bethlehem. So few had readily believed that Mary's little baby was the long-awaited Messiah, yet these Magi had believed it.

Joseph and Mary could count the believers on their fingers. Other than Mary and Joseph, Mary's cousin Elizabeth was the first. Elizabeth had blessed Mary from the moment she heard Mary's voice call out in greeting before Mary's pregnancy was even visible. Elizabeth liked to claim that her baby John was the first believer. The unborn miracle child of old Zechariah and Elizabeth had jumped for joy in Elizabeth's womb at the sound of Mary's voice. Then Elizabeth was filled with the Holy Spirit and sang Mary's praises.

The first ones to believe after Jesus' birth were the shepherds, who visited him in the stable. Next were two elderly people whom Joseph and Mary met in the Temple at the time of their purification following Jesus' birth. According to the Law of Moses, Mary, having given birth to a son, was ceremonially unclean and not allowed into the Temple for forty days. Because Joseph, rather than a midwife, had attended at the birth, he, too, was ceremonially unclean. So both went through the purification process, each bringing a pair of doves to the priest as a sacrifice.

At the Temple Joseph and Mary met Simeon, a devout man who actively looked forward to the coming of the Messiah. The Holy Spirit had revealed to Simeon that he would not die before he had seen Him. The Holy Spirit directed Simeon to go to the Temple while Mary and Joseph were there. When Simeon spotted the baby in Mary's arms, he instantly knew this was the One.

While Mary and Joseph were talking with Simeon, an elderly prophetess by the name of Anna came by. She overheard the blessing that Simeon spoke over Joseph, Mary and the baby as well as the prophetic words he spoke to Mary, and immediately believed that baby Jesus was the Messiah. Because Anna was in the Temple night and day, she knew which ones were looking for the Messiah, and she told them about the baby. One look at the baby's obviously poor parents, and people dismissed Anna's claims.

Elizabeth and her baby. Her husband Zechariah. Some shepherds. Simeon. Anna. Outside of those few, nobody believed that Jesus was special. Everybody agreed that Jesus was an unusually good child, never throwing a tantrum or screaming in anger, but that didn't prove he was God. What would it take, Mary wondered, to convince people that the Messiah was here? When would he step into the public eye?

Yet these Magi – so humble and gentle in spite of their education and obvious wealth – had traveled from afar to worship her child. Various priests and rabbis who lived nearby had, from time to time, heard that Mary had given birth to the Messiah, yet they never came to worship him. They simply didn't believe it.

How had the Magi – Gentiles – picked up on clues about the Jewish Messiah which those who studied Hebrew Scriptures for a living had missed? What did the Magi have in common with those who had believed – such as the shepherds, and Simeon and Anna?

Mary believed because an angel spoke to her in broad daylight. Joseph believed after an angel spoke to him in a dream. Angels also spoke and sang to the shepherds.

Mary's cousin Elizabeth was sensitive to spiritual things because she had experienced a miracle herself, having become pregnant in her old age. Having been struck dumb once for disbelieving an angel, Zechariah, Elizabeth's husband, didn't dare disbelieve again! And John, son of their old age, was the forerunner of the Messiah.

But Simeon received no announcement from an angel. Nor did Anna. Nor did the Magi. None of them experienced miracles. The Magi saw the miraculous star only *after* they believed.

Did they have anything in common? Mary and Joseph wondered.

Simeon, they knew, was righteous and devout. And he was waiting for the Messiah. As a result, he was a candidate for the Holy Spirit to reveal that he would see the Messiah in his lifetime.

Anna spent day and night in the Temple, fasting and praying. No wonder that when she overheard Simeon, she, too, believed.

Was that what made the Magi wise? They were devout enough to leave their homes, one as far away as China, to pursue the truth. And, as Liu Shang had told them, they followed Daniel's example and prayed to ShangDi, the Emperor Above, regularly. In answer to their prayers, God Most High had opened their eyes to understand Daniel's prophecy and to see the star.

"I am amazed," Mary said to Joseph, "that with all the hocus-pocus in their occupation, the Magi were able to sort truth from fiction. Even more amazing is that they acted on what little they knew."

"It reminds me," commented Joseph, "of what the Lord said through the prophet Jeremiah. 'You will seek Me and find Me, when you search for Me with all your heart.'"[13]

They continued walking in silence for a while, each lost in thought.

Finally Joseph broke the silence.

"Wise men still seek Him."

Star of Mystery

Star of mystery, what were you?
    Foretold 1400 years previously
    by Balaam,
        a sorcerer!
        torn between God and Mammon.

Star of mystery, what were you?
    Mystery to scientists
        centuries and millennia later.
    A comet?
    A planet?
    An alignment of heavenly bodies?
    An angel??

A star? But what a star!
    Led Magi from afar
        to an infant King.
    Appeared. Disappeared.
        Appeared again.
    Started. Went ahead.
        Stopped.
    Right over *His* house!

A star? But what a star!
    Brought exceeding great joy
    To the Magi
        who followed
        who believed
        who worshiped.

A star? But what a star!
    I see it.
        I follow.
            I believe.
                I worship.
    Exceeding great joy!
      What a star!

               – by Elsa Henderson

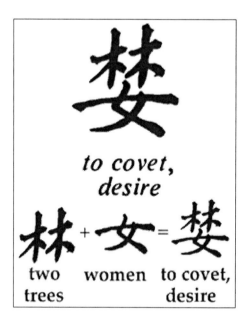

ten; completion   man; human; person   tree; wood

COME

Note the THREE persons 人 in the character COME. (There is a Big One in the middle). Note also that the position of the Middle Person 人 is lower than both the persons on His side.

This illustrates perfectly what the Bible says in 2 Corinthians 5:21: "*God made Him Who had no sin to be sin [offering] for us, so that in Him we might become the righteousness of God.*"

"*... They crucified Him, and with Him two others – one on each side and Jesus in the middle." (John 19:18)*

"It is finished!" (John 19:30)

Chinese 'books', called **bamboo slip,** originated during the Warring States period of the Zhou Dynasty.

Starting from about the fifth century BC, we begin to find examples of writings on bamboo strips. The strips were prepared in advance and tied together with strings to form a roll, then characters were written with a hard brush or a stick on the bamboo surface.

With new media came new content: along with historical and administrative writings, the bamboo strips contain the earliest manuscripts of famous Chinese philosophical texts. Beside bamboo, texts were also written on wooden tablets and silk cloth.

The First Emperor of Qin, who unified China in 221 BC, standardized the Chinese script. Before that time, each of the many states in China had their own style and peculiarities which meant that, although mutually comprehensible, the scripts had many deviations. The First Emperor introduced the Qin script as the official writing, and from there on, all the unified states had to use it in their affairs.

In about the 4th century, the bamboo slip was replaced by paper.

Endnotes

[1] About 400 miles.

[2] Ur of the Chaldees was also known as Ur Kasdim, named for descendants of Arpakhsad, grandson of Noah. The priests in Arpakhsad's line were called Kasdiym (short for Arpakhsadiym), from which we get the name Chaldeans. Arpakhsad's best known descendant is Abraham.

[3] Numbers chapter 31, especially verse 49.

[4] Joshua 13:22

[5] Li is a unit of length which has varied considerably throughout Chinese history. During the Han dynasty it measured 415.8 m or about ¼ of a mile. Today one li measures exactly 500 m.
The Chinese name for the Great Wall, "the Ten Thousand Li Wall", was not intended to indicate a literal distance. The number "ten thousand" is used figuratively in Chinese to mean any "immeasurable" value. Ironically, the actual length of the final Great Wall is roughly 13,000 modern li – or 3,000 li longer than its name's proverbially "immeasurable" length.

[6] James Legge, *The Notions of the Chinese Concerning God and Spirits*, Hong Kong, Hong Kong Register Office, pp. 24-25, 1852. The entire prayer reads much like a prayer one would find in the Bible.

[7] Daniel 9:24-26

[8] Isaiah 9:6,7

[9] Devore, *Encyclopedia of Astrology*, p. 366.

[10] Three O.T. prophets referred to the coming Messiah as the Branch – Isaiah (Isa. 11:1), Jeremiah (Jer. 23:5-6; 33:15-16) and Zechariah (Zech. 3:8; 6:12-13).

[11] Daniel 12:10

[12] Micah 5:2

[13] Jer. 29:13, NKJV

9 781613 792933